Kids Say the Greatest Things about God

Kids Say THE GREATEST THINGS about God

A kid's-eye view of life's biggest subject

DANDI DALEY MACKALL

Tyndale House Publishers, Inc.
Wheaton, Illinois

Library of Congress Cataloging-in-Publication Data

Mackall, Dandi Daley.
  Kids say the greatest things about God : a kid's-eye view of
life's biggest subject / Dandi Daley Mackall.
      p.   cm.
  ISBN 0-8423-2009-1
  1. God—Miscellanea. 2. Children—United States—Religious life—
Anecdotes. 3. Children—United States—Interviews. I. Title.
BT102.M243 1995
230'.083—dc20   95-9295

This book is dedicated to
my own children:
Jenny, Katy, and Dan

CONTENTS

Introduction

All about God

Who Is Jesus?

Talking to God

Ready for Heaven

Telling about Religion

Good Things, Bad Things

Family and Friends

Mysteries of Life

INTRODUCTION

Jesus prayed, "O Father, Lord of heaven and earth, thank you for hiding the truth from those who think themselves so wise, and for revealing it to little children. Yes, Father, for it pleased you to do it this way!" (Matthew 11:25-26).

Children have a truly fresh view of life. They are ever questioning, seeing, and understanding things for the first time. When we grown-ups grow bored and cynical, children can reacquaint us with life—if only we will stop and listen. I interviewed hundreds of kids, ages two to ten. What follows are their profound answers to my simple questions.

My thanks to Art Linkletter and his legacy of listening to children, respecting them as whole people with worthwhile thoughts and ideas. And thanks to all the children who gave me their time and their insights. Way to go, guys!

All about God

WHAT DOES GOD LOOK LIKE?

"**H**e's ever so handsome."

"**H**e looks wonderful, like he could really do miracles. And he's clear, like a ghost, so you can look through him."

"**H**ow am I supposed to know? You gotta use your imagination. He's indivisible."

"**G**od has many kinds of hair, but he keeps them short."

"He has a gray beard. He's at least a hundred years old. That's why it's gray. Used to be brown."

"My grandma has a picture of God, and he wears a robe just like Grandpa's."

"He looks a lot like Jesus, but with a mustache."

HOW OLD IS GOD?

"Older than my mom! Honest."

"41"

"350"

"100 million"

"He's really, really, really, really old. And he never looks a day older every time you see him."

"God is as far as numbers go.
He's too old for age."

WHAT DOES GOD DO ALL DAY?

"**W**alks on water."

"**H**e lives. He lives."

"**S**ame as us, only in heaven. And he does it better."

"**H**e organizes heaven, sending heaven people down here in cloud elevators so they can help us earth people out."

"**M**ost days he builds boats. All kinds of boats. Nobody knows why."

"**G**od watches over us all the time. He has lots of eyes—like spiders."

"**H**e works on clearing off prayer lists people give him. And he answers prayers of little babies because we don't know what they're saying."

WHAT DOES GOD CREATE?

"**G**od makes bees with little wings all day. Probably out of mud."

"**G**od made Jesus first. Then he let Jesus die and be planted in the ground like a seed. And the rest of us people grew up from Jesus seed."

"**H**e makes grass a lot of the days. That takes up a lot of hours. You ever see how many pieces of grass there are?"

"In the beginning, God created heaven and earth. Now he just does people."

HOW DID GOD CREATE THE WORLD?

"Well, he started out doing plants and water and worked his way up to people."

"God had help creating the world at first. Jesus helped him and somebody else I forget."

"God worked on light for about six days. Then he just started shouting the words, like 'Trees!' and there was trees."

"In the beginning, about ninety-five years ago, God created the Pilgrims and the Indians. Then he made Mary and Joseph. And the rest is history."

"In the beginning, everything looked yucky, like when you put cheese in a glass of water and stir it up. Then God made the world and people. But it took sixty-two more years for him to make cars."

WHY DID GOD CREATE THE WORLD?

"So us kids would have a nice place to play."

"He had to create trees or our environment and eco-system would be in serious trouble now, wouldn't it?"

"God kinda got bored up in heaven by hisself. It was too dull. He's very creative."

"**A**dam and Eve started fighting, so God quick made the rest of us."

"**F**irst God tried making only one thing. He did a good job and was very proud of what he made. So he kept going."

WHY DID GOD MAKE KIDS?

"If you didn't have kids, you'd never get parents or grandparents. See?"

"It's the only way to have lots and lots of people."

"God made kids so we could have friends to play with! Otherwise, you couldn't get nobody to sleep over."

"God loved us even before he made us. But he had to make us to prove it."

WHAT MAKES THE CREATOR SAD?

"Like when his creations don't turn out too good—like my big brother . . . or cockroaches."

"The devil makes God sad because he's just so mean. And it makes God even sadder if you like the devil."

"God gets sad when you say bad words (like <u>hate</u>). He hates that."

"When you smoke and drink beer. But the saddest God gets is when people don't make Jesus be in their hearts."

Who Is Jesus?

WHO IS JESUS?

"Aw, you know—Mary and God's boy."

"Jesus? He's the one who makes clay, then adds powder, then shakes it all out, rubs it all around—and we become real."

"What, like you never saw Christmas before? He's in that."

"Jesus? Nobody here at this school with that name."

"Jesus is God, only with real fingers and toes."

WHAT DOES JESUS LOOK LIKE?

"He looks just like clouds."

"Long hair, brown beard, no shoes, on cross."

"Jesus looks just like my sister's boyfriend, only my mom hates him."

"He's very jolly, and he stays in his robe and slippers."

"If you really want to know what Jesus looks like, go to church. They have pictures of him."

DESCRIBE JESUS SO I'LL RECOGNIZE HIM WHEN I SEE HIM.

"Jesus is about a foot long, chubby, no hair, and squirmy."

"He's the most beautifulest person on earth . . . for a boy."

"If I had to describe him, I'd say pockets. He has lots of pockets. And when he takes his hands out of his pockets, they have scars in them."

"He's skinny, wears shredded blankets, hangs his head, and is on a cross."

"He looks like a king and sits in a chair, looking powerful. But don't worry about recognizing him. He'll know who you are."

WHAT DID JESUS DO WHEN HE WAS A CHILD?

"He played with the animals in that manger."

"He had to skin his father's sheep in the fields by night."

"He battled warriors with his superpowers! Then he fought the evil dragon with his bare hands and beat off monsters with his mighty sword!"

"He may have been God's only son, but he still had to go to school."

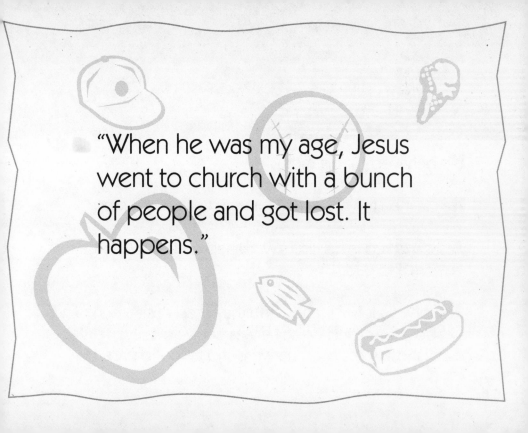

"When he was my age, Jesus went to church with a bunch of people and got lost. It happens."

WHAT DID JESUS DO WHEN HE WAS YOUR AGE?

"He behaved for his mom."

"He cleaned the house and carved stuff out of wood."

"Jesus worked in his dad's workshop and built a house for his mom and dad."

"Jesus had a lot of friends, and they used to sit around and talk about love. And when he was twelve or eleven or ten, one of those three ages, he went and talked to preachers."

"Jesus played a lot with his toys, especially stuffed animals. He just loved stuffed animals."

WILL JESUS CHRIST COME BACK TO EARTH?

"**N**ope! He's already seen enough."

"**H**e's not coming back because it's much, much nicer in heaven. He will just wait for us there."

"**J**esus will come back every Christmas to all good little girls and boys."

"**W**hat do you mean Jesus is coming back? Nobody ever tells me anything!"

"Yes. Jesus is coming again, and this time he's bringing God with him!"

WHAT WILL IT LOOK LIKE WHEN JESUS COMES AGAIN?

"Jesus will appear in the sky in a fiery chariot, but he won't quite look like himself. He'll be a lot older."

"Christians will hear trumpets. And everybody else will hear bugles they play when soldiers die."

"Jesus will come back and set everything on fire except us, if we're lucky."

"**A**t the perfect moment, the sky will unwrap, and Jesus will come back wearing a beautiful gold crown of the finest material. Over his shoulders will be a lovely prayer shawl of fine lace and silk, with everybody's name embroidered on it. On his feet will be sandals of the purest leather. And wait till you see what the angels wear!"

Talking to God

HOW DO YOU TALK TO GOD?

"I say, 'You are one nice man!'"

"You can always reach him at dinnertime."

"You just say, 'Thank you, God, for something to eat. Thank you, God, for something sweet.' But don't say it with your mouth full."

"I think you're supposed to wipe your tears on his feet. Or something like that."

"I always ask God for all the stuff Santa Claus can't come through on."

"You're supposed to pray for what you need—not for what you really want."

"Mostly you just ask other people to pray for you."

WHAT'S THE PROPER WAY TO PRAY?

"Hands together, fingers pointed, folded hands, bended-down knees. And don't open your eyes until they say, 'Amen'!"

"If you're Catholic, you gotta kneel down on boards. If you're regular, you just keep your eyes shut and don't lean on the bed."

"You hold hands with anybody in the room and make a big circle, like duck, duck, goose."

"I usually pray on the phone. Not on the phone to God! On the phone when I'm talking to somebody else, like Grandma or Grandpa, but I get bored. Then I talk to God and just keep saying uh-huh to people."

WHAT DO YOU THANK GOD FOR?

"You gotta thank God for the good things God does."

"I thank God for everything—except beer and drunk drivers."

"I thank God for his little boy, Jesus, and for Jesus' mommy . . . uh . . . uh . . . Mrs. Mary."

"Peoples made cars and footballs and television and skates and clothes. So I just thank God for myself, 'cause nobody else could have made me."

DOES GOD TALK?

"Not unless you're crazy."

"God does talk. He talks in our minds. Only not mine."

"Well, of course God talks! I pray to him at night. He's not going to just stand there and not answer. That would be rude."

"God talks to you way down deep in the bottom backside of your head. So when other people scream at you in the front of your head, you can't hardly hear God."

"**G**od talked to me. He shouted, 'Emily, don't do drugs!'"

"**W**hen I'm bad, God tells me to say I'm sorry."

"**A**s far as I know, God only talks to the baby-sitter."

WHAT DOES GOD SOUND LIKE?

"**G**od talks Bible talk. So sometimes you might not quite understand him."

"**G**od says three things: yes, no, or maybe."

"**G**od talks in Jewish."

"**I**t sounds a little bit loud. Sometimes when God is talking, we think it's only thunder."

"**L**ots of times God talks so very soft that nobody hears him except for really old people who are all by theirselves."

"**G**od sounds an awful lot like my dad."

WHAT DO YOU THINK YOUR PARENTS PRAY FOR?

"They pray they lose weight."

"They pray they win a million dollars in the lottery."

"They pray for toys, just like us, only different toys."

"**M**oms and dads pray that they could have good little children who are as good as they were when they were little."

"**M**y mom doesn't have to pray. If she goes to a big church, they've got a man who does it for her."

DO ANIMALS PRAY?

"**N**ot most of them. Only cows."

"**D**ogs pray for a special dog to come along. Or for you."

"**M**onkeys pray for bananas. Rabbits pray for carrots. Bees pray for honey. Dogs pray for a thousand bones. Bears pray for a fish. Cats pray for cat houses."

"Every single animal prays to live. So God makes them alive."

"Sure animals pray. It's only just that God don't have time to answer their prayers. He's busy enough with people's."

HOW LONG DOES IT TAKE TO GET AN ANSWER TO PRAYER?

"About a minute."

"Sometimes a few days."

"One and one-half hours."

"Oh, years."

"Two very long nights."

"**A**bout 6 million years."

"**I**nfirmity."

"**Y**ou really want to know how long it takes? OK, I'll tell you. Nobody knows . . . nobody knows."

"**H**e's usually answered it before you asked, or at the most, one second after. It's just that we're too stupid to see the answer written all over our face."

"**I**t takes a half hour because you have to worship first before you can ask for stuff."

"It takes four years to get your prayer answered. I know because I asked for a dog when I was three, and I just got one."

"God takes only one day to answer your prayer in the summer, and eight days to answer in the winter. Only he takes forever if you're asking for a Barbie doll."

"I prayed for a boa constrictor, but I never got one. I think it's because my mom hates snakes. And she's prayed longer than I have."

WHY DOES IT TAKE GOD SO LONG TO ANSWER OUR PRAYERS SOMETIMES?

"God can't do everything in a flash, can he?"

"You have to wait until you're dead to get to heaven so he can tell you the answer."

"That's for true! It takes a very long time to get your prayer answered. It doesn't take God very long to do something about it. But it takes a long time for your words to travel through the sky and get to God."

"Almost everybody asks him at once, so it takes about a week to get through. Then it takes twenty-four hours to make your wish come true because he's open twenty-four hours a day. But then, even after your wish is true, he still has to send it down to you."

"When you ask God something, he don't like to do it right away for some reason—that's his own business. But if you wait, he'll get there."

WHY DO YOU THINK GOD MAKES YOU WAIT FOR AN ANSWER TO YOUR PRAYER?

"You're not the only one praying, you know!"

"Clocks work different in heaven. It feels like a long time to you, but if you was in heaven, it would be a teeny, tiny time. It's something like a thousand years is one of our days—or something like that."

"He's very old. Maybe he forgets?"

"Sometimes you think you're waiting, but he's done and said no."

"It's not like he's out on vacation or something. He has a lot to do and no time off. And he's entitled to a life of his own. He's not your slave, you know."

"I don't usually have to wait for stuff. God thinks about it before I do and gives it to me before I even ask him. Now that's service!"

"Sometimes God will wait for a spell because he knows you're going to change your mind soon as he does it."

Ready for Heaven

HOW DO YOU GET TO HEAVEN?

"**Y**ou fly for eight and a half hours on an angel's back."

"**Y**ou fly for one hundred minutes in a spaceship. Or Jesus can take you in just a minute."

"**S**omething inside you turns into a spirit and comes out of you."

"**G**od is dressed up kind of like a ghost. And at the funeral when there's flowers all around you, he'll take you up with him when nobody's looking."

"Your body doesn't get to go to heaven. But you ask Jesus in your heart. And he can tell from the inside if you're saved in your soul. The whole business takes one or two days."

"They bury you in the ground, and you go straight down through the ground to heaven. So I don't know why everybody thinks heaven is up."

"Oh, you get to heaven in a big, black limousine that goes really, really slow. I saw it in a funeral."

"Angels carry you up to the first cloud. Then you have to bounce after that."

"When it's time for you to go up to heaven, God comes down, takes your soul, shakes out the sin, and leaves everything else behind."

"I've heard a lot about how you end up in heaven, and it's very tricky. There's a tunnel and a bright light and something about a train. And you have to fight your way through everything to get to Jesus."

"God flies down to earth for you so you don't be scared. I think that's a nice touch."

IF YOU WERE GOING TO HEAVEN, WHAT THREE THINGS WOULD YOU TAKE WITH YOU?

"Space suit, space helmet, space food."

"One cousin, one rocket launcher, and snacks."

"A seat belt, my pet bear (not alive), and a blanket."

"Apples, oranges, and bananas, but I might not stay long."

"**T**wo cars and one bike. You don't need a driver's license there!"

"**I**'d take a motor-controlled turbojet, a missile nuclear-powered fire activator . . . and my birthday."

"**R**ice and broccoli casserole, a sleeping bag, and air."

"**I**ce cream, a blanket, and a nightgown."

WHAT'S HEAVEN LIKE?

"There's like this big banquet with turkey legs and pudding and potato chips and ice cream and cake. And you get to eat and eat all day. And there's all kinds of refrigerators that stay open. And you can eat whatever you want. Except there's no junk food. God hates junk food."

"In heaven you got your gold houses and people with rings. So it's kinda like down here, except more gold, and all the people are dead."

"They've got sparkly lakes and clouds and schoolhouses just like mine."

"You just wait! Heaven is so great, you want to lean down and shout, 'Hey, Mom and Dad! When you die, be sure and come up here!'"

"Heaven is like Disney World . . . without the sweat."

"OK. Remember how great Christmas was? Well, it's Christmas every day in heaven!"

WHAT DO PEOPLE DO IN HEAVEN?

"Whatever they like. That's why they call it heaven!"

"Everybody helps everybody all day long. And there's no nights."

"Sometimes they fly around and watch us . . . and laugh their heads off."

"When you fall down in heaven, your knees don't get scratches. And there's no major climbing because you're already up there!"

"There's a lot of hugging going on. Mostly you just enjoy your afterlife."

"In heaven you can go places . . . and never get lost."

"In heaven your parents aren't always so busy."

WHAT DON'T YOU DO IN HEAVEN?

"You don't watch TV. I hope I live to be a thousand!"

"You don't never have to go to the doctor or the dentist. I can't wait!"

"If you're in a wheelchair, you can get rid of it up there."

"You don't talk no more when you get up to heaven. You just go around singing all day."

"When you get your room in heaven, you don't have to share it with any of your brothers. Or, if you do have to share, God makes you so you don't mind sharing."

WHAT DO YOU PLAN TO DO IN HEAVEN?

"**W**ork. Everybody has jobs. I'd have a job carrying lambs. I know, because everybody's job in heaven is carrying lambs."

"**I** will help the children of the world through the perils of school."

"**I**'m going to follow the signs that say THIS WAY TO GOD. Then I want to read his tattoos. God's got all our names written all over him."

"The first thing I gotta do is sit down with God and go over all the bad things I did on earth. That may take a very long time."

"If God will let me, I'd like to ring the bells that give angels their wings."

"I'm going to live pretty much like I do on earth. They say people in heaven barely know that they're dead."

WHAT IS THERE TO PLAY IN HEAVEN?

"You can play with your dead pets. Even squished roadkill will be all well again!"

"You can play with real stars and suns and moons and lightning rods."

"In heaven you can play anything and do anything you want . . . except get sick and die."

"You can play with Jesus and God."

"You can play hopscotch on golden sidewalks."

"In heaven you can play ice hockey. I can't play down here because I'm too little and ice melts. It won't melt in heaven, and it's soft."

"You can play baseball and not be the last one to get picked for a team."

IF YOU COULD TAKE THREE PEOPLE WITH YOU TO HEAVEN, WHO WOULD YOU TAKE?

"I'd take my mom and my dad and my middle sister, not my big brother or my little sister. It would be a great trip—better than it was to the Ozarks with all of us in the car!"

"I'd take my mom and my dad . . . and I guess I'd have to take my baby brother because he does so much want to go to heaven."

"I'd take my dad and my sister . . . and a sandwich."

"I'd take ice cream, my mom, and my dog . . . and, if they'd let me take four things, my dad."

WHAT'S SO GREAT ABOUT HEAVEN?

"I think I'm going to like it up in heaven because you know everybody there. Down here I hardly know anybody."

"You can play with wild animals there. And I'm going to ride me an octopus!"

"In heaven there are streets of gold, and you can play right out in the middle of them without anybody running you over."

"**A**nimals talk!"

"**N**obody ever gets chicken pox!"

"**Y**ou won't need glasses or hearing aids or flippers in heaven.

Telling about Religion

WHAT IS THE BIBLE?

"It's kinda like an instruction booklet."

"The Bible is what God wrote in red letters."

"It's the before-and-after life of God."

"It's like stories, but with Bible verses."

WHAT DOES CRUCIFIXION MEAN?

"Crucifixion is how God fixes everybody up."

"It means God hates sin but loves you a lot."

WHAT DOES RESURRECTION MEAN?

"It's when you get a Christmas tree that you plant back in the ground so it will grow and not die anymore."

"Resurrection is what Jesus did right after he died, and right before he put the crown on his head."

WHAT'S A PROVERB?

"An action word."

"It's the word they use to start the Super Bowl."

"A proverb is some kind of computer game. My brother has it."

"It's a kind of an animal."

"Something that helps you do math."

WHAT'S THE GOLDEN RULE?

"Be cool. Stay in school."

"Keep your mouth shut while the teacher's talking."

"I know this one! Pay the electric bill first!"

"It has to do with gold—like give your gold to the poor, or you won't get anymore."

"**D**on't hide food in your dresser drawers."

"**K**eep your hands and feet to yourself."

CAN YOU NAME ANY OF THE TEN COMMANDMENTS?

"**B**uckle up for safety!"

"**D**on't smoke in the bowling alley."

"**D**on't drink beer."

"**L**isten to your parents and do what they said to do. Unless they said don't do it."

"**B**rush your teeth!"

"**P**ut your jammies on each and every night because it's a wrong commandment to sleep without your clothes on."

"**G**et dressed on time in the morning. And don't forget your hair!"

"**D**on't go in to work on Sundays. And if your boss says she'll fire you, call in sick."

MORE COMMANDMENTS . . .

"**M**ake your bed. And it doesn't count if you can see the sheet poking through the bottom."

"**F**loss."

"**C**lean your room on Saturdays."

"**D**on't copy."

"**O**bey your mom and dad. And don't be jealous of God."

"Don't steal. Don't even want it in the first place."

"Don't hit people if they hit you first."

"I think 'Don't kill' is one. But maybe not."

STILL MORE COMMANDMENTS . . .

"**D**on't eat when you have a fever and feel like throwing up."

"**D**on't go in other people's yards."

"**T**hou shall not stab."

"**D**on't sue people."

"**S**ay no to drugs."

"**S**ay no to strangers."

"**H**ave a little peace each day."

"**T**hou shalt not wish."

"**D**on't park in nonparking signs."

"**D**on't mess with other people's stuff."

"**G**ive honor and don't kill your parents."

Good Things, Bad Things

WHAT'S THE DIFFERENCE BETWEEN BAD AND GOOD?

"Bad is loud; good is soft. Bad is big; good is little. Bad is fun; good is not fun. Bad is me; good is my sister."

"Bad is when you beat somebody up and then run away. If you're good, you don't run."

"**G**ood is God, and bad is the devil."

"**I**'ll tell you the difference between bad and good.
You do one, you get in trouble. You do the other,
nobody notices."

WHO'S THE DEVIL?

"His last name is Satan, and you don't want to know who he is!"

"The devil lives in an underground room where you'll go if you're mean—kinda like the basement."

WHAT ARE ANGELS?

"**G**od's little helpers who play the harp."

"**H**eaven people."

"**A**ngels are just good people. If you're really, really, really good—like you died saving somebody—you can become an angel."

WHAT DOES THE DEVIL DO?

"The devil gets to capture you if you rob a bank or kill somebody or shoot guns at children . . . or don't go to church."

"When your soul falls down to hell, the devil is the one who catches it."

"**H**e's a big temptation bug! He whispers in your ear, 'I know your mama said don't play in the street, but go get your skateboard. That street looks good to me.'"

"**S**nips at your heels."

"**M**akes the world noisy."

WHAT DO ANGELS DO?

"They fly from cloud to cloud and bounce off clouds and hide from airplanes so's we can't see them when we fly."

"They have to sit on your roof and listen so they hear what you said about God when you were praying. Then they fly back up to heaven and tell God every word you said."

"They watch you when you're sleeping."

"They pull people out of burning cars and out of quicksand, and keep people from being shot or falling out of airplanes, and help you with subtraction."

WHAT DO ANGELS LOOK LIKE?

"Girl angels wear long, white dresses, and boys wear short, white skirts."

"They wear those round things on their heads . . . five golden rings!"

"They don't look that good because they're all dead."

Family
and
Friends

WHAT MAKES GOOD FRIENDS?

"Friends fight fair."

"A friend asks you 'What's up?' when they see you at school."

"When you both get in trouble, your friend won't walk away and leave you there."

"Good friends don't try to act like they're your best friends, because they already are."

HOW DO YOU HELP OTHERS?

"**I**f it's your folks, you keep out of their hair."

"**I**f they're old, you take them to the other street."

"**B**y pulling weeds."

"**D**o anything without them telling you to do it a thousand times."

WHAT'S SO GREAT ABOUT YOUR MOM?

"**H**er macaroni and cheese."

"**W**hen my mom gets sad, I tell her to think happy thoughts—like her next birthday's coming up."

"**M**y mom brakes for butterflies!"

WHAT'S SO GREAT ABOUT YOUR DAD?

"His chocolate chip cookies."

"His smell."

"You can wrestle him without breaking him."

WHO'S THE BOSS AT YOUR HOUSE?

"My dad is boss 'cause my mom said so."

"My dad is the boss . . . until Grandma comes over. Then he's just one of us."

"I promise, my mom is the boss of our house! She's so good at it, she's even the boss of her work!"

"Girls are boss. We've got 'em outnumbered seven to one."

"All of us are boss—only in a certain order, with my brother first and my dad and me last."

"The real boss at our house is our cat. You should just see us when she meows to go out and we all race to the door!"

DO YOU WANT TO BE A PARENT WHEN YOU GROW UP?

"**N**o. I'm having too much of a good time being a kid now. But thanks."

"**N**o. It's just too expensive to raise kids these days!"

"**N**o. I plan to just be a grandmother."

"**Y**es. I want to be a parent so's I can see what it's like on the other side of loving your kids."

"**Y**es. When everybody gets on your nerves, you can just make the whole world go to bed early."

"**Y**ou bet I do want to be a parent! I want to stay up late and go shopping and work . . . but I don't want to have any kids."

"**I** would have to say yes because I'm very fond of small babies, and I'd have lots of them, but no brothers and sisters."

TELL ME ABOUT YOUR GRANDPARENTS.

"My grandma and grandpa have a whole refrigerator with nothing in it except candy and prunes."

"We never knew my grandmother. She died before my mom was born."

"I love my grandpa. He plays catch with me."

"My grandpa is ninety-eight years old. When he wasn't ninety-eight, he was beating the Chinese people in the first earth war."

WHAT'S THE DIFFERENCE BETWEEN PARENTS AND GRANDPARENTS?

"**A**t Christmas and birthdays it works like this: Parents give presents; grandparents give money."

"**G**randparents get overgrown skin, and the colors fall out of their hair."

"**Y**our grandmother's cookies come out of the oven, and your mother's cookies come out of the bag."

"**M**y grandparents get to eat all the sweets they want because their teeth live in a glass."

"Grandparents are closer to heaven."

Mysteries Of Life

WHAT'S LIFE ABOUT?

"Life is about wrestling the wind—sticking your arm out the car window and wrestling the wind!"

"Life is hard, like in the song: My country, 'tis of thee, sweet land of misery."

"**L**ife is like getting lost in one place after another—the library, Wal-Mart, Kmart, grocery stores, all over the place."

"**L**ife is like being alone, only somebody's watching you."

WHAT ARE MIRACLES?

"**W**ishes come true."

"**W**hat happens when you stand outside with your fingers crossed and say, 'Starlight, Star bright . . . I wish I had a boyfriend tonight. Or just a pony.'"

"**M**iracles are when you do stuff like heal leopards."

"**U**nbelievable things."

"**I**f the doctor does it, it's no miracle. If you do it without a doctor, it is. Like me. I had chicken pox, but just look at me now!"

"**A** miracle is when you do something you've never done before."

"**A** miracle is something you wanted to happen, and it happened without you knowing what happened."

"**F**og. Now there is one big miracle. Think about it."

WHAT HAPPENS WHEN YOU DIE?

"When you die, you go to the hospital and never come out."

"People do all sorts of stuff to you when you die. They get you a box, called a coffin, and a funeral with lots of people and food, and a grave with grass and flowers. And then when they're all done with you, you get to go to heaven."

"When you die, you go to a big, blue square filled with fog. The gate is black, but the rest of the place is white."

"You don't have to get buried if you don't want to. You could get burned or put in a bowl or blown over water or thrown out of an airplane."

HOW ARE BABIES BORN?

"God makes the baby, see. He puts it in an egg and gets it in the mother somehow. Then he makes it grow. When it hurts like crazy because the kid tries to kick its way out, then they go to the hospital."

"I did know how babies are born, but I forgot. I think they are baptized."

"OK. There's a big circle, and then a lot of little worms aiming for the circle. The one that wins gets in the circle and becomes a baby."

"**D**addies have to kiss mommies. Then babies grow inside the mommy for about two years until the daddy can pull it out. It's very hard to pull the baby out. My brother weighed fifteen pounds, and they thought he'd never come out!"

"**W**hen a baby just gets started, they tie it with a cord to the mother's belly button. And that's what you use to pull the baby out."

"**S**ometimes the baby won't pop out. Then they have to cut it out—cut the mommy right open. If that happens, they put a bag over the mommy's nose because she just can't take it anymore."

"I'm not sure how babies are born, but I think it has something to do with the baby-sitter."

"I'm not supposed to talk about it. But they don't grow on trees!"

"I don't know about other babies. I can only say what it was like for me. It was very dark in my mother's stomach, and I had a feeling somebody else was in there with me."

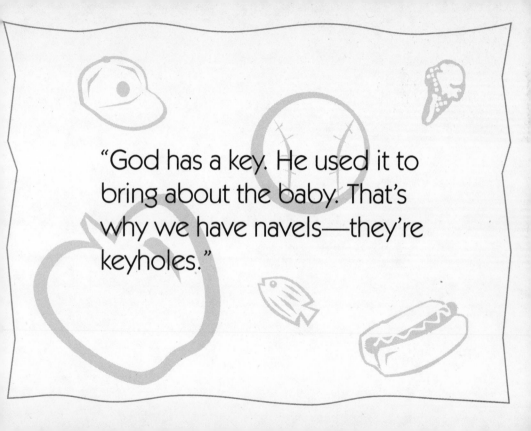

"God has a key. He used it to bring about the baby. That's why we have navels—they're keyholes."